CW01617586

To Katie & Matthew

Poems are like snapshots — —
capturing the scene, saving the essence,
reaching the soul.
Enjoy Poems, they make you think

Memories are mind images, your life history,
treasure them, nurture them, keep them safe.
Enjoy Poems, they aid the memory.

[signature]

May 2002

(The Snowflake pg 97)

TALES FOR THE YOUNG

poetry today

Tales For The Young

Edited by Natalie Nightingale

First published in Great Britain in 2002 by Poetry
Today, an imprint of
Penhaligon Page Ltd, Remus House, Coltsfoot Drive,
Woodston,Peterborough. PE2 9JX

A Catalogue record for this book is available from the British Library

ISBN 1 86226 634 4

Typesetting and layout, Penhaligon Page Ltd, England.
Printed and bound by Forward Press Ltd, England

Foreword

Tales For The Young is a compilation of poetry, featuring some of our finest poets. This book gives an insight into the essence of modern living and deals with the reality of life today. We think we have created an anthology with a universal appeal.

There are many technical aspects to the writing of poetry and *Tales For The Young* contains free verse and examples of more structured work from a wealth of talented poets.

Poetry is a coat of many colours. Today's poets write in a limitless array of styles: traditional rhyming poetry is as alive and kicking today as modern free verse. Language ranges from easily accessible to intricate and elusive.

Poems have a lot to offer in our fast-paced 'instant' world. Reading poems gives us an opportunity to sit back and explore ourselves and the world around us.

Contents

Genny, Eleven And Leader Of The Quartet

She's the leader of the orchestra,
commands and gives her all;
her players in turn support her well,
all within her thrall.
It's difficult to know just why
she enjoys such mighty sway,
she's diminutive and very quiet
and scarcely four-foot three!

Andrew A Duncan

Mouse Without A Tail

Dad came home with a shovel
and flushed him out of the sawdust,
chasing him like a *Tom & Jerry* cartoon
from the shed and across the patio.

His last shuddering stab speared his tail
clean off and he would have finished him off
there and then, had I not cried for mercy.

Fed on bread and cheese -
and milk ladled in on a medicine spoon,
I nursed him back to health,
before setting him up in his own little house
made from matchboxes and sealed
with a tacked-on felt-roof.

After that, he accompanied me everywhere -
school, church, football on a Saturday afternoon
in his very own blue and white scarf.
His favourite was to perch in my shirt pocket,
where he could feel the reassuring beat
of my heart and keep well out of the way
of forgotten boiled sweets and used hankies
that had an unpleasant knack
of finding their way into my trouser pockets.

Thinking about it now,
I've concluded he must be a magic mouse -
for all this happened many years ago.
Yet still he sits on my shoulder,
reading this as I write;
his tiny white whiskers brushing softly
against my own.

Andrew Detheridge

Go To Sleep

My child, it is late
Rest your weary head
Lift your heavy feet
And go upstairs to bed

Go put on your pyjamas
And remember to brush your teeth
And lie on the floor beside your bed
And check the bogeyman isn't beneath

Remember to lock your window
So Jack Frost won't bite your toes
And cover up your head, my child,
So the goblins don't pull your nose

Keep your teddy by your side
As you try to sleep tonight
And pray that he will keep you safe
From the nightmare man tonight

You have nothing to fear, little one,
These things do not exist
They are childhood worries
That can vanish with a kiss

I'll come and say goodnight
I'll make sure that you are fine
I'll come, sit and talk to you
We'll recite old nursery rhymes

So go to sleep in your bed
Don't be scared of the dark
For when you wake in the morning
I'll take you to the park

Sarah Patterson

The Little White Bear

It was now Christmas Eve and the toy shop would soon close
In the window sat a polar bear with a big, black nose
Last minute Christmas shoppers were still bustling here
and there
But nobody noticed the little bear, wouldn't anybody care?

There were now only a few toys left, inside up on the shelf
But the polar bear sadly sat in the window, all by himself
All the other toys had been sold for the special day
The little bear remained, was this where he would stay?

Soft white fur and a big black nose, he thought that he was cute
I'm sure someone would have bought me, if I'd worn a Santa suit
All he wanted was to make a child happy, just to be held tight
To be wrapped and delivered by Santa, on Christmas Eve night

Across the city a mother had been searching for such a toy
A cuddly polar bear, the dearest wish of her little crippled boy
Weary and tired, she suddenly stumbled across this the
final shop
Delighted at what she saw, at last her search could stop

The bear couldn't believe his luck at being wrapped so prettily
Then placed directly underneath, a fairy-lit Christmas tree
The little boy filled with joy as at last Christmas day arrived
Being given the package he couldn't wait, to see what was inside

As he touched the soft white fur his excitement grew and grew
Hugging the bear so tightly, both their Christmas dreams had
come true.

Linda Brown

The Boy

'John, take a shower, you smell,'
His mother yelled.
John, eleven years old and very cantankerous
Likes to hear his own voice, whinged and rebelled
Lay down on the floor, moaning and groaning
Kicking and screaming, language colourful
Warned by his mother, big tears rolled down.
'Dirty knees, mucky face, nothing wonderful
About this son of mine,' she groaned in despair.
'Why me?' she thought as she looked at this boy
Who hated water, never used soap, her son and heir.
This lovable rogue, who wouldn't wash
Didn't like to be clean. If you mention he showered
Created one hell of a scene.
'Why me?' she thought, as she threatened and bawled
'To the shower this minute, or you're grounded again.'
Grumbling and fumbling, John climbs the stairs
Banging doors, moaning, he at last gives in.
Hissing and spluttering the shower he starts.
His mother relaxes, asks, 'Why is for John to
be clean a sin?'

E Hollis

Children At Play

The snow glistens on the ground,
Children play and run around,
Snowball fights and shouts of glee,
Then they spy the Christmas tree,
Tinsel glistens, lights twinkle,
They watch the deer go running by,
Christmas Eve will soon be here,
Presents, sweets, pop and pud,
To fill their tummies
With all things good.

M Roberts

Anticipation

Children's wonderment
Father Christmas
Busy time of year,
Rushing here, rushing there
When what you've asked for
Not quite right
It's just that Santa's
Had a very busy night.
Santa can make mistakes
Having so many places to go
Giving someone else gifts
You've asked for yourself
Gives other child your treat.
Which ever way
You look at it,
No need to blame Santa,
For your Christmas
Will be made complete.
Father Christmas very tired,
Now off home to sleep.

Rosemary Sheridan

The Outwitted Guest

Spider spinning web so fine
To welcome all her guests to dine
Nothing is spared in spider's quest
To lure another would be guest
She does not even need a sign
To say to all do please come in
To sit at table all prepared
Not knowing you have been snared
With strong silken thread so fine
For too late you are entwined
At this there is no turning round
For you are now so truly bound
And alas too late you realise
That though you're invited in to dine
You do not like the bill of fare
In fact you've lost your appetite
Now that you are the main course
In the welcoming spider's lair
And you do not want a single bite.

K K Campbell

A Scarecrow Went A'Wooing

A scarecrow went a'wooing
Which a scarecrow shouldn't do
And he hoped he'd find a maiden
In a field 'neath skies of blue.
But he found no lovely maiden
And that really made him sore
So he jumped about with anger
Thus, he lost a bit of straw.

A scarecrow went a'wooing
Which for scarecrows isn't wise
And he hoped he'd find a maiden
If he only used his eyes.
But although he searched the forest,
Plus the lakeside and the shore,
No maiden came to join him
Since he'd lost a bit more straw.

A scarecrow went a'wooing
Which a scarecrow finds quite hard
And he hoped he'd find a maiden
In the farmer's muddy yard.
But although he asked a farm cat
Who was sharpening a claw
He found no pretty maiden
But he lost a lot of straw.

A scarecrow went a'wooing
Which a scarecrow shouldn't try,
And he hoped he'd find a maiden
If a diamond he could buy.
But he hadn't any money
And just left a trail of straw
Till his insides were all outside,
Now that scarecrow is no more.

Richard J Bradshaw

The Kite

A mischievous breeze, not a cloud was in sight
The right sort of day for flying a kite
The lad's happy laughter, a playful pup's bark
Two very good pals are away to the park
Soaring in splendour in this fresh breezy day
When a sudden strong wind plucked the kite away
Jerked up to the Heavens away from the land
Rudely kidnapped from the young fellow's hand
Dipping, twisting, floating on high
Free as a bird in the blustery sky
Hurried along on a powerful breeze
Bobbing and sailing way over the trees
Slipping down to the meadow where a mare flicks her mane
Skimming hedges and ditches through a cool country lane
Caught in a gust, light-hearted and free
Sailing over a ship on the glittering sea
As he reaches the shore, the wind falls to a sigh
Gliding and spinning as tall trees he passed by
In slow motion dream, just a whisper of sound
His tail torn and ragged, he fell to the ground
A boy with his mother in the still evening light
Gave a shriek of delight on finding the kite
Gently lifts it and carries it home with much care
To Dad's shed - in the morning the tail he'll repair
Where did you come from, to where will you go?
If you could but talk, I would so love to know
One blustery morning, when the wind is on high
You'll be free once again to sail through the sky.

Barbara Davies

Prince Toad

A sad little story about a boy called 'John Bond'
While out looking for tadpoles, fell into a pond.
He scrambled out of the pond, his clothes really soaked
When from out of the reeds, a mother frog croaked;
'Serves you right,' said Mother Frog, croaking with glee
'Those tadpoles you seek, are baby frogs, belonging to me.'
'I was not going to harm them,' said little John Bond,
'I love to watch them swim about all over the pond.'
Talking with Frog, mud on his trousers, felt such a load
Putting his hand in his pocket, pulled out a toad!
'Frog may be their mother who puts them to bed,'
Then croaking really loud, 'I'm their father,' he said.
'If you kiss me, a toad, without making you wince,
I'll turn you into a toad instead of a prince.
Being a toad is far better than being a fish,
You can then watch tadpoles as often as you wish.'
So he did as toad asked and gave him a kiss
As a toad, to be a boy again soon was his wish.
Watching tadpoles, his favourite pastime, he liked a load
Only next time 'A kiss' he'll choose a prince, not a toad!

T W Denis Constance

A Spot Of Bother?

A girl picked up a frog, it gulped and gave a croak,
She closed her eyes and kissed the thing and hoped it would
turn into a bloke,
Preferably of the princely kind, dashing, rich and hunky,
Frog puckered up and closed his eyes at approach of
ugly monkey
Girl opened eyes and was most upset
At the titchy thing a'quiver still in hand
In fairy books things such as this turned out
'Happy ever after' sort of planned.
Frog too was non-impressed, beast had half sucked away his breath
He tightened springy legs then hopped away half frightened
still to death,
The girl then rubbed her tingling lips, they somewhat seemed
to oddly burn,
No! Tingle! Sparkle! Spangly hurt, some folk just never learn.
'Oh God,' she uttered as a spot popped up with an eruption of
Vesuvian proportions,
Her wishful dreams of romance and fortune now nightmarish
performing wild contortions,
As a wart sprung up of an ugly kind she'd never
once intentioned,
Frog meanwhile thanked his old mum's remedy for getting
rid of his unsightly lumpy blemishes.

George Robinson

Listen And Learn, Please

Children do you know what the word means to 'enjoy'?
Is it to switch TV on or get the biggest, most expensive toy?
Do you think about creation or who did all those things?
Trees, lakes, fish, seasons, birds and bees with wings.
First he put light, then dark, also made the Earth into a beautiful park,
Put a pair called Adam and Eve who sadly Satan did deceive.
So listen to some wise advice from God above,
Who is very kind and full of love,
He cannot be seen but has spoken from above,
Sending Jesus, his dear son, down with advice.
All he asks is for people to be peaceful and nice,
Show loving kindness which costs nothing you see,
To have good morals, be honest, truthful and kind,
What chance do you have, for Satan is definitely snaring young minds,
His food, drugs, filth of various types, thinking you will get a hype
Beware, this is not a joke, sadly it is true,
So listen to your parents' warning, they love and want the best for you!
Because one day you will be parents too,
Wishing you had listened I can assure it's true,
Experience comes from the heart so this message is for you,
Whether between the ages of ten, fifteen or twenty-two!
Listen and learn.

Esther White

Warmth By The Tree Of Secrets

Open your heart, open your arms, it won't do any harm.
Open your ears, open your eyes, take those around out
of the dark.
Give a little kindness, give a little smile
'Cause in the end, it's all worthwhile;
Under 'the tree of secrets.'
There's an old willow tree, its branches hang low
Shading the spot where the boys and girls used to go.
What a tale it would tell if only we could hear
Of the two little boys and two little girls it saw each day
for a year.
Their lives were quite different, but best friends they became,
The tree bears the scars where each one carved their name.
They all were so lonely and got on from the start,
Their friendship was timeless, they never would part.
The tree watched them play, and scream and shout,
No one knew they met, they must not be found out.
For Charlie and Linda were rich children
And Mark and Samantha were poor children,
But girls had the bedroom, boys slept on the floor.
The days they flew by till a year was nearly over,
Mark and Samantha knew they would move soon, once more
be a rover.
The tree watched their farewell, the leaves they were weeping,
They moved on one morning while the others were sleeping.
How happy they were, they would never forget their
friendship that year,
Each time they remembered, they would both shed a tear.
The tree knows the secret, has its autumn leaves scatter,
It's not the things you possess, it's the friendships that matter.
To us, it is about our kids, because when they give us a smile
Or a big hug, it puts life into perspective and reminds us
Of the simplest, most important things in life.

All dreams come true, the children met up.
They got married; Charles to Samantha, Mark to Linda.
You can have nothing, yet have it all, as we've found out.
Having no money needn't mean you're not rich.
Your tree of secrets!

V Borer

A Cautionary Tale

There was once a computer who had a name,
Its name was Barnaby James.
It never liked maths or arithmetic,
It only liked to play games.

The children adored Barnaby James,
It filled their lives with delight,
They tapped its keyboard all day long,
Even into the night.

Barnaby James was the children's friend,
They played with him all the time,
But now they've grown up they can play Solitaire,
Yet can't count from one to nine.

M Reynolds

Suzy

I had a little dolly called Suzy,
She went for a walk in the park
She played on the swings and the roundabout
And when she came home it was dark.
I put her to bed in her little cot
And wrapped her up nice and warm
She snuggled down with her teddy bear
And didn't wake up until morning
I dressed my little dolly called Suzy
In her pretty party dress
With bows in her hair
And buckles on her shoes
She was the prettiest little dolly
That anyone could choose
I took my little dolly to a party
With her buckles, bows and party dress
She was the prettiest little dolly there.

C Isaac

The Plight Of Clara Clutterbuck Entwistle

Now Clara Clutterbuck Entwistle
Was as bright as a hen could be,
But each time she heard a bell ringing
She flew up in the air nervously.

No one knew why Clara was nervous
They couldn't put a name to her plight,
But bells were becoming a nuisance
Especially if they rang through the night.

Her owner was really quite worried
As he tried to settle her down,
'Tomorrow to the vet's I will take her
To see if a cure can be found.'

Next day she was placed in a basket
In the back of his truck she had fun,
A big bump and the basket opened,
Clara flew up and then she was gone.

She travelled all night without stopping,
She could not find her way to the ground,
If a bell rang she did not notice
But she thought she would never be found.

But suddenly the wind was calmer
And slowly Clara sank to the ground,
She was back home where she had started
But her owner has not yet been found.

They say he's still looking for Clara,
This may or may not be true,
It is said, each time bells are ringing
The sound of a horn echoes too.

Irene Grahame

Mr Snotty

If you ever pick your nose,
the only things you'll find are crows.
Some are black and some are green,
some are too unsightly to be seen.
Some are soft and some are hard,
some you pull out by the yard.
Some stick them underneath their chair,
then go away and leave them there,
and some disgusting little brats
even eat them, fancy that.
I think that it is really gross
to eat the products of your nose.
It really isn't very nice,
it is a quite disgusting vice.
And now that you're past the age of six,
you'll no longer do these dirty tricks.
I'm sure that you're a gentleman
and use a tissue when you can.

Pauline Fletcher

In The Snow

Snow falling softly on every place.
Winter sun sparkling like icing on lace.
We'll have fun in the snow.
Teaching you how to throw,
Making snowballs and then
Hiding in a snow den.

What fun for the moment
With snow crisp and clean,
Before the snowman starts to lean.

We skate and slip
And sometimes trip,
But when all is done,
We really had fun.

Now it's all over, the snow turns to slush,
We have to clean up so here comes the brush.
With fingers so numb and toes all aglow,
It's time to go in out of the snow.

Home in the warm with a bright fire gleaming,
Love, cuddles and a hot drink steaming.
Time for bed now and happy dreaming.

Pamela Bryan

Our Little Mouse

Our little mouse has his own house
He lives in our wood-box outside
He has great big ears and a long thin tail
If he sees us coming he hides
We leave him food when it gets late
On a pile of bricks near his door
Then out he comes with his whiskery mate
To pick up the cheese from the floor
Then indoors they go, Gladys and Fred
To cuddle up and eat their supper in bed.

Rose Horscroft

If I Live That Long (That Is)

When I am old and need a hospital bed
I will try to behave, but it's easier said.
I shall call for the nurse and pretend it's not me
And ask for a bedpan and then not wee.
I'll swig other patients' Lucozade and eat their nut whirls
And then blame the night nurse, 'The one with the curls.'
The scent of violets or lavender I will not wear,
And I'll not let anyone perm my hair.
I'll not eat mince or drink milky tea,
Nor crochet, nor knit or watch soaps on TV.
Frilly nighties and slippers are not my style,
Nor dried flower arrangements, I think they're vile.
The People's Friend I will not read,
But I will drink gin and get totally peed!
I'll sit on the commode for an hour and a bit,
Then get into bed and promptly - shit.
I'll store biscuits and grapes down my stocking leg
And throw talc on my face, so I look nearly dead.

Now, reading this you may think I'm a sod,
But, what the hell? I'm waiting for God.

Marilynne Connolly

My Little Friend

(To Summer from Devin)

I've got a little friend
She really makes me laugh,
I love going to play with her,
We've even shared a bath.
She's always trying to kiss me,
She really hangs on tight,
And then she tries to bash me up,
One day, we'll have a fight.
I really think she's funny,
She is my little friend.
Do you want to know her name?
It's Summer, my little friend.

Suzanne Thomason

Solomon's Jews

Solomon had a fling
She was from the land of identikit features
Where they lift their skirts high to dance,
Rucked above their knees – and faces . . .

Converts walk the Negev Desert
But in Solomon's day
A fling or two was enough
It guaranteed a green card to the promised land

Bring a rucksack full of nectar
And a bit of cotton-fluff popcorn
And gods will grin and let you enter –
Well actually, gold would be better
And you've plenty of that in Africa.

Solomon was a great judge in his day,
Well actually, a bit of a realist and minimalist
Nevertheless, we hear of him still.

The Israeli SAS stormed in
And took Solomon's children out –
Did he really manage all of them?

There was a king in Africa not so long ago
With several hundred kids, not goats – children.
Old Solomon did his bit too
For ancient old Israel that is.
(So now we know why they're so stuck up,
an African said)

Old Solomon had a fling or two
And so they grew and fought.
Now we have to separate them, brother from brother,
In memory of that great affair.

Did the Great Queen really produce
Or was she having old Solomon on,
As ladies have been known to do!
It's an old cry, you know,
'It's yours . . .'

Anyway,
Solomon's Jews have gone to the Promised Land
As promised.

Fletcher Bounty

Blanket

Blanket yellow and bright,
My closest friend
Through my short little life.
My comfort when I needed you
To snuggle up to,
When I needed a friend.
Now you're all faded,
But still my closest friend.
Only at night times,
When I close my eyes
And you take me with you
To a different land,
With sugar and spice
And all things nice,
That's how I always know you're mine,
Beautiful yellow blanket of mine.

Laura Stinchcombe-Sorrell

Sibling Sis

Parents both loved dearly
Mother and father
Just the same.

But then if you are a son
Eldest or not . . .
A love as fundamental
Is also sown . . .
Before your life has barely begun.

It's a generation thing
Concerning that other sex
The stork more often brings.

Along with all those fairytale stories
Of queens and kings;
There is that one of a princess fair
Without worry or care
And you know why?

Because you are the lesser known of prince
Who for her
Is in a protective way
Like background action . . .
Found to be there.

Though as the years progress
And she the opposite begins to impress
With her air of confidence
And self-composed dress . . .
Become a hindrance from the start.

Though by her reassuring smile
You know still
And always will
You are equally contained within her heart.

Malcom Peter Mansfield

The Fairy

I spied a fairy hiding
Behind a large green leaf,
A tiny delicate creature
My eyes stared in disbelief.

So tiny and so delicate,
She peeped out at me,
I sat as still as marble
Beneath the willow tree.

She danced and skipped and floated
On tiny gossamer wings,
Then delicately drank from a drop of dew
And then began to sing.

It sounded like a tinkling stream
Or a gentle sighing wind,
I held my breath as she came close by
And settled on the children's swing.

'Hello!' I said in a gentle voice
So I would not frighten her away,
'Good day,' she trilled and curtsied to me,
'My name is Merrie-May.

I like your pretty garden,
I play here quite a lot,
But now I must away for tea,
Before they think I'm lost.'

I shook my head a little,
Had I dreamed that fairy song?
No! I really did see her,
Because she left her fairy wand.

One tiny little daisy,
Wound round a willow stick,
With stardust dusted on it,
To grant me perhaps a wish.

But as I stoop to pick it up
It vanishes before my eyes
And tinkling melodious music plays,
Then slowly fades and dies.

S P Cockayne

Lauren's Song Of Angels

Sometimes you seem to get lost in this whole world.
You are scared . . . at first, you seem to see
how much you have to run
from your enemy . . .
The world is cruel, the world is bad.
It is *I* who can protect you . . . always.
Come with me, I can help you, always.
Can't you see?
I can take you to a world of rich, cool waters,
A place full of clouds, a place where angels fly.
You'll see.
Don't turn your back on me at all,
Don't turn your back on me.
On me . . . at all.

Lauren Sammout (9)

Who'd Be A Worm?

Worms are long and sleek and wriggly.
How they love the wet and cold.
That, I think, must be the reason
Why most worms do not grow old!
Worms don't seem to get arthritis
Though their beds are cold and damp,
Which is just as well because they'd
Shrivel if they used a lamp!
Earthworms never seem to sneeze much,
Though they have no clothes to wear.
Somehow they can manage nicely –
But I wonder how they dare!
Knives and forks are not included
In an earthworm's etiquette.
Neither table, chair nor sofa
Have they learned to use as yet.
Earthworms need no soap or water,
Bathing worms are very rare.
Worms don't use a brush or comb 'cos
Worms don't have a head of hair.
What an awful shame it is that
Earthworms cannot talk or sing,
Never in a church can marry,
Though they have a sparkling ring!
Crawling on a shiny belly
Really can't be very nice,
Think how cold their bellies must be
When they're crawling over ice!

Joan Tompkins

Holidays

It's a serious business a holiday
Lots of equipment necessary, you see
Buckets, spades, rubber rings
The obligatory lilo for me.

It's a serious business a holiday
As we march along the beach in time
Dad leading the expedition, us in the middle
And Mom carrying the gear, at the back of the line.

It's a serious business a holiday
Staking out our claim on the sand
With cool bags, ice boxes, drinks and goodies in store
Up goes the tent, ready to be manned.

It's a serious business a holiday
Now the towels are laid on the sand
Parasol and deckchairs positioned just so
Most of the gear in our hands, ready to the sea we go.

It's a serious business a holiday
Splashing about in the sea, lolling about on the lilo
Dad rowing our inflatable boat
The one paddling is me.

It's a serious business a holiday
Playing games with bat and ball
Then covering ourselves with sand
Building sandcastles, digging deep holes
While the ice-cream drips down our hand.

It's a serious business a holiday
As we troop off back to the hotel
Suntanned, overheated, full of food and
Totally tired as well.

Katherine Parker

Children

Children bring magical moments
Into each and every day
A smile each little gesture made
Endearing moments to last always
Then as they learn
You teach them well
Your knowledge gained through time
A hug and all the love you have
Just grows, each kiss divine
The character your child will form
The wonder and delight
The energy he will possess
From morning until night
You want so much
Give even more
Wish days would last forever
And as the years begin to flow
They were the best days ever.

Jeanette Gaffney

Crocodile

Mmmm. It's hot.
I like it when it's hot.
I need the sun's heat on my back
In the morning.
Later, when the sun is high,
I slip into my local pool.
Like you I like to swim and float
Just keeping my nostrils and eyes
Above water level.
I like to see and not be seen.
Sometimes I rest in the long grass
On my flattened space
Shaded by a nest of tall reeds, hiding.
People say I'm lazy,
Have filthy habits, cruel,
But as a rule of thumb
I wash every day
And have my teeth tested
On a regular basis.
My favourite food is red meat.
Nature burgers I call them.
If I'm hungry I'll look for food and eat.
I never wander far away.
Come to think about it,
Don't we have a lot in common?
If I was a boy I think
I would be Huckleberry Fin.
Perhaps you would like to be me.
I don't have to go to school

John Burns

Summer Dream

In warm summer weather,
We stood together,
Penny and I in the park;
We looked at the swings
The seats were all bare
No one was there
I said, 'Let's have a lark
And see how high we can go.'
High, then higher and higher we flew,
Shoulder to wing with the birds we knew,
A bright red kite for the wind to toss,
A gull as big as an albatross.
That's high enough now, but oh, we can't stop!
See, oh see, there's a chimney pot;
Hold on to it, we've had enough
It's dusty and sooty and rough;
I called to Penny, she wasn't there,
I felt myself falling I knew not where;
Down and down and round and round
Then a bump as I reached the ground.
Beside me was the wooden seat,
The park seat where I'd been asleep.

M M Mose

Lucy Lush

Lucy Lush had hair like a brush
All stiff and bristly and brown,
Although she had two big pink bows
They looked so silly with her big red nose,
She thought she was so prim and proper
Then out came her tongue and on jumped a grasshopper.

Wibbling and wobbling like a clown
She pritted and pratted around the town
First in one shop, then the other
She really was quite a bother,
Telling people what to do
What to wear and where to go.

The dogs and cats all hid from her
Because she liked to curl their hair
Pretty bowties about their neck
Top hat and gloves, oh so yuk,
'Come here, Kitty, Kitty,' she called out loud
'Let me dress you up and twirl you around.'

Now Lucy Lush loved to dance
But oh dear me, all she did was prance,
She tried to sing like a nightingale
And it came out like a banshee's wail,
She cried and cried and stamped her feet
Then disappeared down a hole in the street.

Mary Neill

I 'Wannabe' A Grandma

I 'wannabe' a grandma and know all there is to know
then when the clock said schooltime, I wouldn't have to go,
I'd know my sums and spelling and how to sew and knit
and always have an answer – when I was asked for it.

I wouldn't have to go to work 'cos that's what Granddad's for
I'd sit at home read magazines then bake pasties by the score,
there'd be paper, pens and sticky tape for when the children came –
to settle down and make things and count me in their game.

At Christmas I'd buy presents for everyone in sight
then deliver them the night before and maybe stay the night;
when morning came I'd stay in bed for my breakfast, toast and tea
and hope that just for *this* year it was after halfpast three.

I'd have a car for shopping and day trips to the sea
and sometimes ask my grandchildren to come and stay with me;
I'd cook their special dinner and special chocolate cake
and fill their little bellies with as much as they could take.

I'm so glad to be a grandma – oh how the years have flown!
those little babies I once held – like me are fully grown,
I loved the times they visited – and the quiet when they'd gone
and pray their children do the same when at long last *they're one.*

Jim Pritchard

Sweet Tooth

Candyfloss and toffee
Bubblegum, gobstoppers too
Chocolate cake and sticky things
Are not really good for you

For each contains some nasty things
That work both night and day
Like gangs of little miners
Attacking teeth to cause decay

When you are young, your teeth are too
So caution should be heeded
If you don't protect your teeth
The dentist will be needed

In his chair you'll sit alone
Awaiting needle or gas
To numb the sensitive area
Hoping extractions are not en masse

When time is right you're told to
Open your mouth so wide
Then the dentist hovers over you
And a nurse stands by your side

Stale breath, it seems to engulf you
You stare up at nostrils flared
Then the drill starts to penetrate
And you wish you'd really cared

He strikes the nerve, you want to scream
But your mouth is full of tools
You only have yourself to blame
You've ignored the basic rules

Clean your teeth both night and day
And especially after meals
Or you will pay the ultimate price
And know how an extraction feels

Protection is far better
Than false teeth in later life
And the time you spend in the dentist's chair
With its pain and unknown strife

So stay away from sweet things
Protect your teeth and gums
And go through life with one full set
A second chance, it never comes!

Francis Farmer

First Steps

Little child, safe in your mother's arms
Little child, blessed be your charms
Little child, Fate's hostage in an unsafe world
Your tiny toes they'll uncurl

To walk next spring towards the rising sun
Into a barren land hard won
In hope penury to withstand
Or face adversity in a life not grand.

If you do go astray,
You'll find a way
That's not a hopeless bind
But to the young useful-kind.

Little child, you'll learn to pray.
Let not dark horizons you dismay.
Tho' caught in Fate's rough seas
You'll escape her stern decrees.

Angus Richmond

Shadows At Bedtime

Lying in bed, watching the shadows
Leaping all over my room
Is that a dragon with fiery breath
Or maybe a witch riding a broom?
The candle sits and flickers
And makes the shadows look scary
But I can feel safe in my bed
For beside me is my teddy.

Fiona Bazley

The Gumby's

Once upon a time there was a wonderful land
Filled with perfect white mountains and valleys.
It was here that the Gumby's lived.
In the beginning they were healthy inhabitants,
Pink, shiny and in peak condition,
Now however their homeland was in danger from the
Sugary clan,
Every day vast quantities of disgusting substances
Would pour down on them from the orifice,
At the entrance to their world,
And sticky brown sludge cascaded down the sides of
the mountains,

Then just as the day clock struck twelve-thirty
The Crunch masters would arrive,
Hideous flat yellow monsters in their salt coats,
Who slid over the rough terrain of the interior slide,
And down into the eternal abyss,
It was now a long time since the spike army had been seen,
Who on many occasions previous, were seen at least three
times a day,
Cleaning and polishing with their brushes and paste,
Which always left a breath of fresh air,
Without their arrival things just got worse.

A ghastly smell appeared which made the Gumby's feel sick
And to the inhabitants, sickness arrived.
The mountains were clad in a yucky scale,
The litter from the Crunch masters rotted in the valley,
It was now only a matter of time before the chatters invaded.

The knowledge of them had been handed down by
previous generations
They were called the army of grinders and suckers,
Impostors, white plastic mountains and pink imitations of
the originals,
Called by the odd names of Upper and Lower,
The last Gumby finally surrendered, and the Sugary clan won.

Remember children:
If your toothbrush and toothpaste you do not use,
Then your white, shiny teeth you may lose.

Ann G Wallace

To The Only Child

I was a one and only child
Kept in on wet and cold days
Allowed out when it became sunny and mild

Alone in my bedroom looking out at the rain
Watching the passing traffic
My nose pressed against the windowpane

I'd wish for a sister or a brother
That other children had
So I could play with another

Those days of loneliness are long gone
I married, had five children
A family of my own where I belong

A grandmother of ten
I have now become, no more alone
My days are full of laughter and fun.

Ann McAreavey

Starting the Day

A dancing girl and a little elf
Danced and twirled upon my shelf
In time to music being played
So I raised my head up to the stage.

Tiny folk only inches high
I managed to glimpse through half-open eye
They'd chosen the shelf afacing my bed
Where the view was clear by just lifting my head.

Now fully awake, eyes open wide
Where was the elf and girl I'd spied?
But it seems that in the cold light of day
My eyes had played tricks I have to say.

Yet for an instant a wondrous sight
Two people dancing to their hearts' delight
To see such images of people at play
Makes for a wonderful start to the day.

Sheila Graham

Children All At Sea

Those far away years with us young and frivolous
Yet Mum and Dad heeded us with respect,
How excited when Dad bought a caravan!
The days when 'vanning' was a hazardous event.
Each of us - a duty to perform.

Dad, so cautiously driving,
Requesting for silence, Mum wouldn't overlook it,
Reaching the site, out there the sea,
Tide coming in, my brother with spade and bucket,
All with our 'cossies', couldn't wait to swim.

My brother and I filling, carrying the water barrel,
Mum's sharp recall, other duty to be done.
'Go find the waste-disposal point,
help Dad fit up the awning - run'
makes the caravan double its size.

Then finding new friends in nearby vans
A whole week so deliriously rosy!
Late night time watching moon over water,
Sleeping in the awning, so cool, so cosy!
An early awakening to a thrilling new day.

Near the end of the week, duty, sadness.
Each to our ways of parting;
Names and addresses carefully exchanged;
Journeying home, but memories heartening.
To this very day, it's how I found my best friend!

Jim Lucas

Mr Bun

Mr Bun, Mr Bun,
Terror of the chicken run,
When they see his pointed ears,
All the hens burst into tears.
Hide the eggs and hide the grain,
Perhaps he won't be back again.
Where's Mr Cock, is he asleep
While all the chickens moan and weep?
It's bad enough when little mice
Gobble up the bags of rice,
But Mr Bun is worst of all,
It's trouble when he comes to call.
Never mind, the cows all sigh,
He'll end up in a rabbit pie.

Mary Crowhurst

The Parrot

King David had a parrot
His name was Obediah
He sat beside his master
As he played upon his lyre.
No matter what his master said,
The parrot said the same, he did not tire
This pleased the King no end
And soon came to love his little friend
Until one day the King was cross
Dutifully the parrot replied, the King at loss
He could not say he hadn't said it –
For the parrot's duty, we give full credit
Poor parrot was banished from his master's side
A position revered by many with pride
So remember well, this sad tale of woe
And whatever you say to a friend or foe
May be repeated, near or far
So be sure your message will do good
And help another win their star.
There is one sure thing, 'Our Lord' hears all
He gives us strength to obey His call.

Dorothy Parish

Box Car Racers

Vroom! Vroom! Mind my car,
Box and pram wheels
Grazing knees running – pushing
Skipping girls step aside
Down the hill
Round the corner
Have a spill
Wheel comes off
Pick up the bits
Scratching heads
Hammer and Dad's nails
Shouts and bangs
Off we go
Speeding, skidding
Along our back lanes.

Roy Barker

Web Of Fear

The one creature in this world
That can make my toes curl
Is the one with eight legs?
Spinning those sticky, creepy webs.

Spiders

Even the tiniest catches my eye
Sending swift shivers down the spine
Their hanging homes cling to hair and skin
Heartbeat pumping adrenalin.

Spiders

They seem to be everywhere,
Especially in the bath when I stand bare
Across the ceiling eight legs speed
Causing great terror indeed.

Spiders

This terror I cannot control
Friends and brothers find droll,
But I know men who share the fear
And these monsters cannot bear.

Spiders

Dad; come take it away,
Into the garden out of my domain
Descriptive names even send a chill
Not one of these creatures can I kill?

Spiders

Why do we this innocent fear
Usefully, insects he clears
England has none that bite
Horrific pictures fill my mind of

Spiders.

Evelyn Poppy Sawyer

Blast

In the prehistoric jungles there once lived a creature called Blast;
He was small, quick-witted and he could run very fast.

Blast was one of the Bananatees who loved eating
prehistoric bananas;
They would eat these all the time together with their favourite
prehistoric sultanas.

Blast could smell a lot better than he could see;
From nasty meat-eating dinosaurs, called Loathsomepocoporous
he often had to flee.

The Loathsomepocoporous believed that they were fearsome;
Yet to Blast, they were simply irksome.

Blast had a friend who wasn't as quick-witted as he was and
in danger of being eaten;
Thankfully, Blast was always around to ensure that the
Loathsomepocoporous were beaten.

Their lack of success made the King of the
Loathsomepocoporous very frustrated,
So he made up a plan to trap Blast, but it was very overrated.

A trail of fruit was laid consisting of bananas and sultanas
fragrantly scented;
It was all too much for Blast's friend who into the trap was
foolishly tempted.

Blast ran to the rescue realising it was all a plot;
Surrounded by Loathsomepocoporous his friend was now
frozen to the spot!

With a high-pitched scream Blast caught the
Loathsomepocoporous' attention;
The distraction gave his friend the chance he needed to escape
from his detention.

Back towards their home Blast and his friend began to race;
The Loathsomepocoporous were in hot pursuit but they simply
lacked their pace.

It seemed as usual Blast would reach his home and safety;
Then the ground shook and the Loathsomepocoporous thought
they were in for something tasty.

The King of the Loathsomepocoporous let out a great hiss
thinking that Blast would soon be dead;
Then he was squashed quite flat, as a tree fell down and hit
him 'bang' right on the head.

As more trees fell down the remaining Loathsomepocoporous
rapidly retreated;
Blast and his friend had escaped and their enemy was once
more defeated.

A great asteroid had hit the earth from way out in space;
It was a disaster that no dinosaur was at all equipped to face.

Blast and his friend were however still alive;
And though many struggles lay ahead, in the end they
would survive.

J P Walker

Evening Fairies

Whilst sitting in my garden chair,
Relaxing in the evening air,
I knew the fairy folk were there
Playing around my face and hair.

These evening fairies dressed in blues
To mingle with the shadow's hues,
Had silver wings and silver shoes,
Protection from the night-time dews.

Then clinging to my garden chair
I found a single thread of hair,
Of purest gold, it was so fair,
I threaded it with utmost care.

And using petals from the flowers
I'd gathered earlier from the bowers,
I spent remaining night-time hours
Stitching a quilt with all my powers.

Then, stealing forth at early morn,
When dewdrops glistened on the lawn,
An hour or so before the dawn,
The time another day is born.

There, tucked inside a sweet red rose,
I spied a fairy in repose.
Not wishing then to spoil her doze,
I draped the quilt around her toes.

If you're a lover of the wild,
With mind unspoilt, just like a child,
The fairy folk will come to play,
And if you love them, they will stay.

Till one fine evening, you could spy
A host of fairies flying by,
Attracted by the night-time dews
Just like a cloud of deepest blues,
With gossamer wings and silver shoes.

Angela Douse

The Visit

When we go to see my aunt
(My mum says she's a saint)
She gives me such a hug and kiss
I very nearly faint.

As soon as we get through the door
I must take off my shoes.
I don't know why it's only me,
But how can I refuse?

The adults sit about and talk
While I can sit and play
With Aunty's tabby cat - provided
I don't get in the way.

Then a trolley is wheeled in
With sandwiches and cakes,
Soda drinks and ice-cream too
Topped with chocolate flakes.

Aunty never seems to mind
How much I eat and drink
I only have a little - well
That's what I let her think.

And when it's time to say goodbye
To Aunty and her cat
I leave before she hugs me tight,
Feeling rather fat!

R T Kiel

Playmate

Come out an play in the garden with me
The sun is shining bright
Bring your balloon and I'll gently blow
And you can chase your balloon about
I'll keep you cool as you run along
For you see that's what I do
Can you guess who I am, I'm sure you can
I'm just the wind, that's who.

Sandra McKinnon

Back At Boarding School In The 1920s

The end of term is almost here,
The hols will get a rousing cheer,
But still there are some things I'll miss,
A game of footer is pure bliss!

I'm not a chap who often swanks,
But skill like mine deserves some thanks!
I cannot count the goals I've scored,
The school's good name has been restored!

Why won't things go without a hitch?
I've now spilt ink and need some blitch.
I'll have to ask the nearest chap
To clean this mess down on my lap

Now sometimes I've been known to blub
And even worse, go off my grub,
When after ragging in the dorm
The punishment's beyond the norm.

Some days I show a lack of spunk
And then, of course, I'm called a funk,
But really I've got lots of guts
As I'll soon show these silly muts.

Well, now I need a drop of fizz!
These adverts really are a swiz.
My pocket money's running dry,
I really don't know what to try.

Sedley Andrus

Searching

Where are you going
In your old anorak
With your cheeks aglowing
And your pack on your back?

I'm travelling west
With the sun in my eyes
To find where it sets
In the darkening sky.

Though I walk a quick pace
And don't stop to rest
I'm always too late
When it sinks in the west.

So shall I go east
To see where it's from
And give up the chase
To see where it's gone?

Or leave till I grow
My great puzzling quest
To find where it goes
When it hides in the west?

Will the secret unfold?
Will I catch up at last?
As I'm ever more bold -
No, the world spins too fast.

G M Peplow

Granny Gregory's Alphabet
(with acknowledgement to The Children's Encyclopaedia)

A is for Abigail who Abseiled at Ayr,
B is for Benjamin Brought by a Bear,
C is for Catherine who Came with her Chum,
D is for David who Danced on his Drum,
E is for Edmund who Enjoyed it out East,
F for Francesca who Flambéed a Feast,
G is for Granny, Gone down the Glen,
H is for Henry who Hustled the Hen.
        H is for Hen and I think you'll agree,
        It is also for Hannah who carried a banner
        And danced in the manner of chimps having tea. *
I for Irene who Intends to use Ink,
J is for Joseph who Jumped a high Jink,
        And J is for Jonathan, also for James,
        J is the start of a number of names.
K is for Kate who Kept a large Kite,
L is for Lawrence who Laughed at the Light,
M for Michaela who Marched to the Mine,
N is for Norman, of Newts he caught Nine,
O is for Oswald who an Owl did Observe,
P is for Pia with a Pot of Preserve,
Q is for Quentin who Questioned a Quail,
R is for Robert who Rests on a Rail,
        R is for Robert and also for Rose
        Who Rambled to Ramsgate as everyone knows,
S is for Stephen whose Steed lost a Shoe,
T is for Thomas who Tried a Tattoo
        (not a picture on skin but a roll on a drum
        which tells people to look or listen or come),

U is for Ursula who Upset an Urn,
V is for Vivien with Volumes by Verne,
W for William who Went to the Well,
X is for Xavier who eXpects to eXcel,
Here's Y and Z who declare it a shame
To stay at the bottom without any name.

** Of course, she could dance perfectly well.
She was just having fun.*

Catherine Gregory

When Santa Calls

My mother said that if I were naughty
Santa wouldn't call with the present.
I don't like her when she speaks like this;
It's much nicer when she's pleasant.

She knows I want a motor car
As I've already told her twice,
Red or white with lots of chrome,
You know, something that really looks nice.

I did have a car until lately
But it was old and dented and worn,
I got tired of pushing it down the street
I'm not sorry now that it's gone.

Most people look forward to Christmas
When Santa calls round with the toys,
Everyone filled with excitement and pleasure,
It's one of life's greatest joys.

The waiting and expectation,
It's good to be alive,
After all, my mother is eighty-three
And I'm nearly sixty-five!

A St Clement

Christmas Eve

Now, if you've been good all year long,
You'll get lots of toys,
Cos Santa only brings them
To good little girls and boys.

But if he sees your old toys
Scattered all over your room,
The only things you'll get from him
Will be a shovel and a broom.

So make sure your room is tidy
And your clothes are folded and neat,
Also leave tea and biscuits for Santa,
Not forgetting sugar lumps for Rudolph to eat.

Now after you've said your prayers,
Fall asleep, as quick as you can,
Because he won't have time to talk to you,
Cos Santa's a busy old man.

Jean Hendrie

My Little Cat

Soft as silk and oh so cute
Dressed in a grey fluffy suit
Velvet nose and bright green eyes
He watches me with a look so wise
When I call 'dinner' he pricks up his ears
He comforts me through sadness and tears
Contentedly he purrs with an occasional yawn
He sleeps on my bed each night till dawn
A bushy tail he loves to preen
And the longest whiskers I've ever seen
He loves to loll in the sun when it is hot
Bless him . . . my little cat, the best friend I've got.

Hazel Smith

Personal Pets

My fluffy kitten should be white,
But ash and dust brings different sight;
When there's a chance to roll or scratch,
My kitten, quickly, chance doth snatch.

My furry bunny loves to nibble,
She eats her food without a dribble;
Each day I take her, out on lawn,
She hops and skips just like a fawn.

My smooth-haired mouse likes gentle rub,
He really loves an ice cream tub;
He gently fits into my hand,
He really loves a scratch in sand.

My smoky rat brings fear to some,
One word from me and rat will come;
He crawls across my neck and arms,
For me he never brings alarm.

Each day I share my time with pets,
Each day new targets I will set;
No matter what the worries of day,
My pets will take my cares away.

John Paulley

The Children's Dance

We'll dance in the dawn and through the blue day,
We'll dance like the stars in the wild, whirling spray,
Away on curled waves as they surge up the bay.

We'll dance in the morning when the sun rises high
To the whisper of leaves as the wind rustles by
And the larks pour their song on the earth from the sky.

Then down the cool gardens through noon's blazing hours
Where fountains fall splashing in cold diamond-showers
And freshen the faces of sweet-scented flowers.

We are the children who dance like the light
Dressed as the moon is, in silvery-white,
Frocks fashioned from stars on a fine summer night.

We'll skip through dew till the thin mists rise
And the glow-worm lamps burn green, and the skies
Deepen, rose-gold, as the daylight dies.

We'll fade like pale flowers and turn into dreams
Caught in the gleam of the moon's magic beams
As they shatter on glass of deep pools and dark streams.

When gales come and winter, sad earth wrapped in grey
In a numb, frozen silence we stay hidden away;
But we'll dance through the spring on the first shining day.

Diana Momber

A Children's Night-Time Rhyme

Here is a little story
About a little man
He is only seen at night-time
But, not by everyone.

It's children that he visits
When they have misbehaved.
He shines a light in windows
And knocks upon the panes.

Daytime he's invisible
To every girl and boy,
But sees when you are naughty,
Hearing every word you say.

When you're in bed and cannot sleep,
Although you're very tired,
A face behind the curtain peeps,
Under the duvet you hide.

So children, remember, if you can,
Parents know if you are good or bad.
They can hear the little man,
As his visits make them sad.

Jacqueline Coman

Lilly The Duck

Dancing along the road I go,
I notice all the cars going slow.
I wonder is it because of me?
I don't think it really can be.
Maybe I'll move, just in case,
I don't like the look
On that man's face.
He is waving his fist at me,
So I'm closing my eyes
So I can't see.
I am now dancing on the path,
Safest place,
So don't be silly,
Take the advice
From dancing Lilly.

Alice Devita

Our Bears

In our house, beneath the stairs,
There lives a family of bears.
There's Father Bear, who's big and fat,
And Baby Bear, who's like a rat;
So small and new and wizened he,
His Mummy gives him milk for tea.

We do not see them in the day,
But late at night they come and play
And when I'm snuggled tight in bed
I've sometimes thought the Mother's said,
'They're all asleep, now we'll go out
And play at humans, but don't shout!'

And then from darkness, quiet and meek,
They've sallied forth for hide-and-seek,
While Mother Bear has baked some bread
And Father Bear's stood on his head;
Because, you see, it's cramped in there
For a great big bear beneath the stair.

Patrick Davies

Boys

Dirty face and runny nose
Take of his shoes, see dirty toes.
Shirt unfastened; button missing,
But heart-shaped lips just meant for kissing.
Spots all over; dirty collar,
Just can't whisper - has to holler.
Pockets full of bits and pieces
One look from him - pulse rate increases.
Little, tatty, mucky boy
Why is your heart so full of joy?
What makes you feel you'd like to eat him?
Even when you have to beat him.
Yes! You are a lucky Mumsie
Hug your boy and have some funsie.
Lots of love and sticky kisses,
Oh, the things that Grannie misses!

D Adams

A Kid And A Half

She's a kid and a half, she makes us all laugh.
She knows what to do with her eyes, oh! so blue.
Her look will beguile and you will just smile.
She's sharp as a tack, of brain there's no lack,
She's sometimes a dream but always a scream
And keeps us in fits with her funny ways.

She's a gem and a half, always good for a laugh,
At sixteen months old, she's worth more than gold.
She chatters and chants and still wets her pants,
But what does it matter? We all love her patter.
She keeps us in stitches, we all wet our britches
With laughter at her funny ways.

She powders her bottom, puts rather a lot on.
She is never discreet but always smells sweet.
Her chuckles delight, her smile is so bright.
A dancer she'll be, just you wait and see!
Or maybe she'll sing, but joy she will bring
With fun and her comical ways.

She's a kid and a half, she makes us all laugh,
With meals she's so good, she eats all her food,
She loves peas and beans and eats all her greens.
She strings words together, could go on forever.
She knows what they mean and she steals the scene
And we laugh at her funny little ways.

She's a kid and a half and we all have to laugh.
God knows what she'll do when she's twenty-three,
But you can bet money, she'll still be a honey.
She'll go miles and miles with laughter and smiles,
But to me, she is love, sent from Heaven above.
Truly we're blessed with her lovable ways.

Joanne Quinton

Can You Hear Me Mother?

Can you hear me Mother?
I'm stuck here in the loo.
I've shouted till my voice is hoarse,
Don't know what else to do.

The door's jammed fast, the lock's stuck too,
The window's shut so tight
And even if it came undone,
I'd not jump from this height!

Can you hear me Mother?
Oh please come soon I pray.
The toilet roll's gone down the loo -
This hasn't made my day!

Oh Mother dear, why won't you hear
My desperate cries of woe?
Because I said, 'Don't touch the lock,
You asked why - now you know!'

Paddy Jupp

A Zoo Outing

What a time had the little ones
At the zoo in Fairy Land
Monkeys springing from branch to branch
Acrobating to make them laugh
Lions with their manes in trim
With their families, what a loud din
Pandas eating their favourite meal
Whilst peacocks strut to please their mates
Dolphins jumping up with glee
Out of the water at the perfect degree
Parrots in their bright coloured plumes
Shouting their wares at children with balloons
Ice-cream stall visitors waiting in a long queue
For chocolate ices and lollipops too
The day at the zoo was so exciting
On the way home on the coach
There was everyone making a hullabaloo
At the school gates one and all
Left their mark, by announcing
A present from us all to you teacher,
Miss Pamela Maitland
Then with happy faces
Mums and dads and little ones at home
Fall asleep dreaming of the wonderful
Zoo Fairy Land outing.

Alma Montgomery Frank

Dinosaurs

Millions and millions of years ago,
In the dim and distant past;
Dinosaurs ruled the Earth,
As long as their age did last.

The various kinds of these creatures
Made the Earth their domain.
With their various kinds of features,
In the sun, the wind and rain.

Some dinosaurs were carnivorous,
The same as lions and tigers of today.
Other dinosaurs were herbivorous,
Just like horses and cows that eat hay.

All dinosaurs laid eggs;
Then their young hatched out to be reared.
Like birds and reptiles of today,
Since the dinosaurs have all disappeared.

Some dinosaurs were to be feared,
Even though they were quite small.
But why they all disappeared,
Is a mystery to one and all.

Denis A Walsh

My Angels

The day my babies were born
The very day of birth
Two little angels
Were left upon this earth.

The day of their second birthday
The day that they were two
Two little monkeys
Turned my home into a zoo.

The day of their fifth birthday
They day that they turned five
They changed again to monsters
Surely devils in disguise.

Perhaps when they are older
Perhaps when they turn ten
Perhaps those two little 'Angels'
Will grace my home again!

Sarah Jane Bell

The Puppeteer

There's a puppeteer in our town today
He made them dance, he made them play

Children came from everywhere
To watch the puppets dancing there.

Brightly coloured for all to see
He made them dance so merrily.

I'll be a puppeteer one day
Make the children laugh and the puppets play.

Until that day when my dream comes true
I'll sit and watch him, just like you.

A Fidler

Jack In The Box

Oh what a funny toy I got
Upon my birthday.
What was it? I really couldn't say.
It was a little wooden box
At first I thought it was some blocks.

I rattled it and battered it
Across the floor it ran.
Goodness gracious,
Out popped a little man.

They tell me that his name is Jack.
Is this true, is this a fact?
His home is in this wee, small box
And he does not care for those bad knocks.

You press down his little sprint
When you wish to visit him.
Up with his laughing face he will pop
And I am very sure he will make you hop.

Stella Brown

Pain P.S.

Little Tommy ran to Mum for he had cut his knee,
Said Tommy, 'Make it better Mum, for it is hurting me!'
Mum soon put a bandage on and then to Tommy said,
'Pain is just a message from cuts up to your head.
Brain then gets the message that you've been hurt somewhere,
Then you can go to Mum or Dad and get the proper care!'
But poor Tom's knee still hurt him
And to his mother snorted,
'Why does my knee still hurt so much
Now that it's been reported?'

Ernest Mould

The First Day

These shoes are right! This blazer's small!
This uniform won't do at all!
I think I'd rather run away
than go to school on my first day.

The other kids will all make fun!
I think I'll just stay here with Mum
I'll stop at home now, if I may;
report in sick on my first day.

My hair's a mess – I look a berk!
I'll never understand the work.
What's that? It's nearly nine you say?
Now I'll be late on my first day!

And now the gate is looming near.
I think I'll really hate it here;
I won't know what to do or say.
I'm terrified of my first day.

But who's that there? A friendly face!
Some welcome smiles about the place!
Someone to help me on my way
and show me around on my first day.

I've made new friends. We'll all be mates!
There's lots to do. The lunch is great!
Now perhaps I'd rather stay.
It's really nice on my first day.

Steve J Waterfield

Katie And The Beast

Katie was a baby – a baby tortoise she
Who lived under a heat lamp because she was so wee.
She ate and slept, and slept and ate,
Until that long-awaited date
When she was big and old enough
To face the outside world so rough.

At first inside the house, exploring all around,
She recognised each human and knew each sight and sound:
Then came the day – the exciting day –
She heard her owners' voices say,
'Let's put her outside in the sun,
It's time she had some different fun.'

So Katie looked around, her world had grown so much
With lovely sights and smells, exciting things to touch.
But stop! What's that? Oh, dearie me!
Whatever can that huge thing be?
Poor Katie's had a dreadful fright,
She'd never seen such a fearsome sight.

She drew her head inside her shell, but then she thought,
'If I can't see I could be trapped and caught,
I think I'll take a little peep,
But careful watch I'll surely keep.'
So out she popped her tiny head,
Hoping not to end up dead!

The great grey, hairy beast was standing much too near,
It just might pounce on her, that was her greatest fear.
Her tiny beady eyes peered out
To see if humans were about,
For she felt sure if they were there
The beast to harm her would not dare.

They were!

So Katie bravely stood her ground -
The dog just looked and turned around.

Roma Davies

Ally Finds A Friend

'Come and play with me,'
Said Ally to the cat
'No, indeed I will not,' said the cat
'I am sitting on my mat.'

'Come and run with me,'
Said Ally to the dog
'I am far too tired,' said the dog
'Go and ask the frog.'

'Come and hop with me,' said Ally
But the frog did not want to,
'I'm too busy croaking,' said the frog
'Go and ask the kangaroo.'

'Come and skip with me,'
Said Ally to the kangaroo
'The sun is far too hot,' said the kangaroo
'And I have other things to do.'

Ally asked the birds to play
But they all flew away
'I wish I could find someone,' said Ally,
'Who would come with me and play.'

Ally asked a little tortoise
If he had time to play
'I cannot go anywhere fast,' said the tortoise
'So I have time to stay.'

Ally and the tortoise
Became the best of friends
He found a friend to play with
And here the story ends.

Anne Logan

A Fresh Start (To The Day)

When I get up each morning,
My mother calls to me,
'Wash well behind your ears and neck
and not just where you see.'

I scrub my knees and elbows too
I always wash my feet,
In fact I scrubbed so hard one day,
My left foot looked like meat!

I clean my teeth and between my toes,
I've washed the freckles right off my nose,
I scrub my knuckles almost bare,
My once dark locks are now quite fair.

I have this dream I'll tell to you,
I want to cover my face with stew!
Then through pools of mud I'll slink,
Oh, wish our shower would go on the blink!

At half-past seven I'm fresh as dew,
I leave the bathroom good as new
And Mum says I'm her pride and joy.
If only she'd realise, I'm a five year-old boy!

Jackie Stubington

Cat's Prayer

When I rest alone in bed
(Dog for friend and cat for head),
Remember me, sweet Jesus. Say
'There lies a cat in purr decay.'

Sun may shine and moon may round.
Wise cats eat fish (progress found).
They pace and sound and strut the stage.
All live in a beginning age.

Hair may fall and teeth may rot.
Stomachs explode. Wisdom's not
The most aesthetic of fine ways
To beautify what Time decays.

Whenever you see a cat,
Try to recall the skin that
Placed its body upon a tree
Died, crucified, for sin and thee.

Little child, where'er you are,
Talk to furry cats today.
For Louis Wain once painted cats.
That is all that I have to say.

Hywel Davies

NCP's The One For Me

When Noah set sail in the ark,
Having watched all the creatures embark,
He announced, 'I'll heave to
Close to Ararat Zoo -
That's assuming there's room there to park.

Norman Bissett

Trees

You look at a tree
And what do you see?
Something that's there
And always will be.
In winter, stark, bare,
No flowers in its hair.
In spring softly green
As earth's wakening is seen.
In summer, full shade
For every warm glade.
In autumn regal, bold,
Brown, crimson and gold.
We notice them not
Though they've seen a lot,
Battles, bloody and dread
Before them were spread.
Then they too were brought low
For ships and for bow,
For man does not care
All destruction he'll share.
And for those who stood sound
Then fell to the ground,
Their toil is not done
There's no rest to be won
For man knows the full worth
Of black gold in the earth.
So when you look at a tree,
Mark well what you see,
Cold, barren and ugly without them we'd be.

B G Metcalfe

Spider

I always think it's a spider
that mark there on the wall,
I'd reach it with a paper cup
if only I were tall.

A spider makes a wobbly track
and lives there in the bath,
it can't walk up the sides at all
and leaves no aftermath.

But spiders come and spiders go
they take their mystery with them,
they crawl from room to room and so
I do think I would miss them.

That shivery spider on the wall
is just a piece of plaster,
it looks so real, all black and curled,
but made from alabaster.

Julie Ashpool

Douglas And Donald - Identical Twins

Douglas and Donald like being together,
They go out to work in all kinds of weather;
They shift all the snow from the railway lines
So that the trains can keep to their times.

One day the twins were chugging along,
Huffing and puffing and singing a song;
They were so pleased with what they had done
To make it all safe for the engines to run.

'Well done,' said the others they passed on the way
As they went towards home at the end of the day.
'You've done a great job, you've done your best,
And now you deserve a good night's rest.'

Happy and tired they slept through the night,
Woke up next morning when it was light.
'Come on,' said Donald, 'it's time we started.'
Donald and Douglas don't like to be parted.

Rev D D F Smith

Teddy

There he sits upon the shelf
Like a small, contented elf,
Perhaps in days of old
He was a 'Jolly Roger', pirate bold,
Who ruled the seven seas with fear,
Whenever 'Teddy' did appear.
I got him in 1911,
Just when I was turning seven,
There he sits in my bedroom,
Passed down as an heirloom.
My grandma knitted all his clothes,
He talks to me, or so I suppose
And watches over my repose
With his turned-up button nose.
He's related to all the great teddies in the land,
Queen Victoria gave him her hand.
He came originally
From the Hapsburgs of Germany
And with Princess Alice he's had tea.
So there he sits
And I love him all to bits.
Now he's a bit worse for wear,
A bit tatty and threadbare,
As he sits in my armchair
Yet with no other better bear
Can my 'ted' compare,
And for me he's always there.
A teddy's for the young at heart
A teddy bear will never grow old,
For my teddy's worth his weight in gold.

Alan Pow

Little Train

Little train ran on rail track, thinking as we went his way
Of the scenes he was passing, colourful and very gay.
Driving cab held little driver, in a suit of darkest grey,
Next to him was man to shovel coal in fire to blaze away.
Carriages held little people, some of whom were off to town,
Often using this type of travel, this way had such great renown.
Little children with their school friends in a very special coach
Sitting tightly in their seat, so no other it can poach.
Little mums with shopping basket, plus a fat and shiny purse,
Checking written last reminders, fail to get things would be worse.
Children though enjoying journey, looking forward to their play
Little train goes chugging onward, happy as a summer day.
Little train comes into station, pulling to a grinding halt,
People dismount from the small train knowing driver has no fault.
Then the driver takes the small train little further on its way,
To a siding where while resting it is cleaned with soapy clay.
If you go in any toyshop, there bright colours you assail,
Green and red, blue and yellow, wooden train on metal rail.
Little boys plus adult fathers wind trains and then watch them go
For when small boy asks to try them, hard the dad who answers no.
When his son then tries the train out, this is what Dad longs to do,
Everything his lad is doing, years ago Dad did them too.
Find out which is small boy's favourite, when boy wakens Christmas Day,
Will find Santa Claus has brought it, now can play entire day.
Dad enjoys his dose of childhood, lets go all dignity,
For today he's small train driver, feeling fit and fancy free.

Barbara Goode

A Poem For Children

Down our street lives a nice old man,
With a spade and a fork and a watering can
And in his garden, he loves so
The trees and the flowers grow and grow.
This old man has his own pet dog,
That lies at his feet like a little brown log
And by the roses you will see
A bird in a cage, on the apple tree.
Thin old man owns a ginger cat,
With a long, slender tail that never lies flat
And in the garden by the house
In a hole in the corner, lives a little grey mouse
And if you look there any day,
You will see the cat and the mouse at play.
Around the lawns you'll see them streak
And in the bushes play hide-and-seek.
Each day the man walks up the street,
To buy some bread and buy some meat
And when you see him, you will find,
The dog and the cat are close behind.
We hope one day, when you have grown,
A dog and a cat and a bird you'll own,
But we hope you'll never own a mouse,
Because your mum won't have one in the house.

T E Maxted

Jessica

As the night draws to an end
I go to turn the bedside lamp off

I stop and hesitate and leave it on

She looks so beautiful, I pull the covers up
And rest them on her shoulders
I brush her hair away from her eyes
Her skin so soft and unblemished

I sit down next to her
Not realising time going by
Just sit staring and admiring what I have
And feeling so proud

I love you Jessica,
More and more each day
In everything you do and
Everything you say

Goodnight Jessica

Love, Mum xxx

Angela Wright

Ryan, 'The Angel'

Young Ryan Reece had the face of an angel.
His hair was the colour of corn spun with gold.
His beautiful eyes were a deep shade of violet
And as for his voice, it was out of this world!

Each Sunday morning, he sang in the choir;
Standing in church in a white cotton smock,
But all of the boys from the village would mock him
And said that young Ryan was wearing a frock!

Now, all of this taunting made Ryan unhappy,
Yet he wouldn't let on he was worried, or cared.
For he hatched up a plot that would end all the teasing:
To be put into action, next week, during prayers!

The following Sunday he stood on the front row;
Singing so sweetly as part of the choir,
And took from the folds of his flowing white garment,
A peashooter; loaded and ready to fire!

All of the boys had their eyes shut quite tightly
As Ryan took aim and the peas made their mark.
Then every boy knew that Ryan, 'The Angel'
Was really 'A Devil' dressed up in a frock!

Sandra Wolfe

School Trip

'Off to France,' the teacher says,
There are only a few days
then we'll be in gay Paree,
ten of your friends and you and me.
Remember now to be polite
and if you need to have a bite,
chips and burgers the kids will beg,
no it's snails and a nice frog's leg!
On the ferry, a plastic bag,
Stay near the rail - it's such a drag.
Up and down and up and then
whoops, there goes my lunch again.
Postcards to the lucky few,
Mam and Nan and Auntie Sue.
What a lovely time we're having,
but getting there will seem like heaven.

Cheryl Mann

A Nonsense Rhyme

I set out on a journey
With a chap they call Mad Ernie
And we shopped along the way
At Sainsbury's store
We bought some fish in batter
But it didn't really matter
For we neither of us knew what it was for.
We left the supermarket
In a car but couldn't park it
So we left it in a side street off the square
But my eyes were red and swollen
When we found that it was stolen
For we searched and searched, but no it wasn't there.
With tempers hot and hissing
We just daren't report it missing
As we stole the car last week, oh yes and so,
We'd now got our comeuppance
And it didn't matter tuppence
'Cause we'd had our fun
So now we let it go.
We bought a loaf and honey
But we had so little money
And we would have caught the bus
But didn't dare
For we hadn't got a fiver
And we couldn't fool the driver
So we walked it home and didn't really care.

J C Eaton

Eddy

I dreamt of ancient times so long ago,
My ancestors were wild and really gross,
They had huge arms and legs and liked to show
Their deadly teeth to those who came too close.

I felt I should be true to them and show
How fierce an animal I was born to be;
Yet in my heart I must admit I know
That being beastly really isn't me.

I have a loving nature, all for you,
My greatest joy to feel you close to me,
Just squeeze me tight, the way you used to do
For then I know I'm safe as safe can be.

Have I grown soft? Do I no longer care
That I've become a modern xxxxx xxxx?

Geoffrey Martin

The Snowflake

I watched you float down from the heavens
Large and fluffy and grey.

I watched you land on fence and road
So quickly you quietly lay.

I saw your pattern against my glove
All fancy and like lace.

I saw you linger then melt, in seconds gone
Just moisture on my face.

I heard the sound of easy sweeping flakes
Sowing through the trees.

I heard the silence that you caused
Muffled on a breeze.

I felt your cold breath on my upturned face
An icy finger's touch.

I felt in my heart the joy of winter's sport
Games I love so much.

Jean Selmes

Colours

Red, yellow, blue and white
All these colours shine very bright
When I go out I see lots of colours
Then I look up and see lots of others
I look in a little blue pond
And clearly see more colours beyond
Now it's dark the colours have gone
But dark colours shimmer across the lawn.

Gordon McPhail & Andrew Lamb

A Child's Dream

She fills the house with joy each day
With life aglow,
At different roles she likes to play
Her own side show.

A ballet-dancer - all the rage -
She loves to see -
With grace tiptoes across her stage,
What next to be?

Perhaps she'll be an actress famed
And top the bill:
Whate'er the part as yet unnamed
Your dream fulfil!

R M Shallard

The Princess, The Prince, The Donkey And The Dragon

The young Princess Jo-Jo worked hard at her sums,
She could hardly wait for her holidays to come.
How nice it would be to have some fun,
To go away with her royal Dad and Mum.

Hendra Castle was the place where they went -
In Cornwall, Land of Magic and Legend,
Full of wizards and the occasional gnome
Who had all mysteriously turned to stone.

They were sitting outside their holiday home one day
When a French donkey called Doris came their way.
On her back was the Crown Prince Fred,
A most wizardly gnome who looked very well fed.

'Bonjour, comment allez vous,'
Said the Princess to dear old Doris.
'Bonjour, your Royal Highness,' the donkey replied,
'Get up on my back and we'll give you a ride.'

Jo-Jo jumped up with the Prince, she looked so sweet
As they happily clip-clopped down the street.
Through the green valley, across the silver stream,
Until the Princess let out a very loud scream.

Suddenly with a roar, a pong and a ping,
Up jumped this huge, great, horrible thing.
It was the Deadly Dragon, Dreadful Dick,
With a fiery tongue and a tail ten feet thick.

Jo-Jo screeched and Doris hee-hawed,
Fred made a squeak as the Dragon roared,
'I'm hungry, ho hum! What's this I see?
I quite fancy a nice Princess for my tea!'

You should know that Doris was a Queen among donkeys;
'Not blooming likely,' said Doris at once,
'I'm a world karate champ who always wins
And now I will make you pay for your sins.'

With a swish of her tail and a flick of her ear,
She put Dick flat on his back, shaking with fear.
He cried, 'Mummy,' as Doris made him squirm
Like a tiggly, wiggly, wriggly worm.

The dragon ran off say, 'Ooh, my head aches!'
Crown Prince Fred gave them all ice creams and cakes.
He rewarded dear Doris with a Big Gold Cup
Plus one hundred carrots, and they all cheered up!

George Puttock

Under The Bed

Dad come and save me,
there's a monster under the bed.
Johnny don't be a silly boy,
it's all in your head.

You've woken up twice already,
and it's only half-past ten,
so Johnny go to sleep
and try not to shout me again.

Dad please come and help me,
there's a monster in my wardrobe,
so in Dad comes in his pyjamas
and his silly red bathrobe.

So in the wardrobe he looks
and his eyes roll up to heaven,
now Johnny will you stop this,
it's nearly half-past eleven.

Dad won't you please come and help me,
there's one in my cupboard now,
if this happens again my lad,
you're going to be in a row.

Try not to do this gain,
it's nearly half-past twelve,
you've got to grow up some time,
we all have to sleep by ourselves.

Dad there's one in my bedroom,
and it says it wants to play.
Johnny try to ignore it,
perhaps it will go away.

So dad turns and looks at the clock,
he can see that it's half-past one,
but when he gets up in the morning,
he finds that poor Johnny has gone.

Jeffrey Kelly

To An Infant Small

Dear child enjoy and appreciate your infancy as the years simply
speed by
Let my mothering comfort bring gladness never, ever denied
Let it radiate and shine as you are mine, all mine
When you dream I pray you will be adored as through my
eyes you shine
Dear child as I sit here and ponder by your little bed
What visions do you master in that tiny infant head?
I with loving care and attention alerted by your every move
Dearest darling baby, I hope you will approve

Dear child of mine as I gently rock you and gaze upon your face
I thank God who created thee nine months not in haste
Born to perfection for all this world to see
You are mine and so beautiful as I treasure continually
Dear child I vow to protect you and give comfort when you
are sad
Enjoy your growing up with corrections avoiding bad
Sleep my little angel, I shall always be near
No harm will ever come to thee, sleep on and never fear.

R D Hiscoke

Faces

How many faces have I got?
How many would you like to have?
Four at least; now that's a lot
To have to wash and dry and shave.

Bad enough if you're a fellow,
But think of women's daily chore
Battling with complexions sallow.
A painted face we'd see no more.

But what a lark 'twould be to spy
Before, behind, to left and right
And never have to turn an eye.
I'd whack them all in every fight.

Four mouths, however, would be best
For I could eat and drink together
And use the third new foods to test
While loudly singing with the other.

But you'd have no place for an ear
With faces new on either side.
If fixed upon your chest or rear
You'd feel so odd you'd want to hide.

And if together noses four
Were runny from the common cold
Some slime and snots must reach the floor;
Two tissues only could you hold.

You really shouldn't push your luck.
The Lord above might hear you speak
And fix a face to sides and back
And then you'd be a circus freak.

T Meaney

The Real Father Christmas

When the red fur-trimmed costume
Of Father Christmas with his reindeer
Carrying his sackful of toys
Fades into the children's past
And illusion is shattered by realism
But maturity brings realisation in belief
That he does exist in spirit.
He lives within us and knows
How to grant our innermost desires
If we trust in Him, who
Has our best interests at heart.

V Stamp

My Heart Is Yours

There was no greater joy in my life;
Than giving new life to you;
Like that day when you were born;
You were a real gift from my Lord God.
You are not a toy, but a human being;
You are not here to be ill-treated;
Nor to be neglected or abused;
Like so many children are these days;
You are here to be guided through life;
To be given all my love;
To be taught the ways of peace;
So that you may be given everlasting hope;
Yes my child, love, peace and hope;
You are the future of all mankind;
A gift from my God;
He has led me throughout my life;
Now let Him lead you;
Remember those three words;
Yes, love, peace, hope.

Alf Williams

All Things Nice

Girls are supposed to be sweet and pure like sugar and spice,
It's boys who are naughty, spitting and picking their nose.
Girls made to scream, boys showing spiders, beetles and mice,
Boys get catapults and peashooters, a window gets broken
'It wasn't me - it was her, Mrs Rose.'
Girls help their mums with cooking, boys fling a beetle in the batter mix
And chewing gum stuck on the floor.
Boys like guns, bang, bang, round Mrs Johnson whose gums show through her jaw.
Just then a boy jumps out and a lady jumps out of her bones,
Boys like scooters, girls go slow, watch boys doing wheelies,
Their tyres may explode.
Boys bang on doors and hot-foot it up the road,
Showing sweet little girls slow worms and slimy toads.
Girls have party dresses and ribbons in their hair,
Boys have grubby faces, dirty knees, odd socks and don't care
And are double the trouble in pairs.
Girls play dollies, like Barbie and Cindy, that is gentle.
Boys want rough stuff and evil things that look mental.
All things nice!

Maria Costello

For Callum: Mummy's Little Miracle

(Written for my nephew, Callum Philip, on the day he was born)

Welcome little Baby – we're so pleased that you've arrived,
With your tiny toes and fingers and your beautiful blue eyes.
You're Mummy's little miracle and it's good to have you here;
We pray that you'll grow big and strong, and safe without a fear.

I wonder, little baby, what it's like to be so new;
We've been waiting for so long to hear your fresh point of view.
What would you like to say if you could only speak your mind?
What would you want to talk about?
What new things will you find?

We've so many things to teach you - you have such a lot to learn,
And we will all be proud to watch you grow,
Miracles at every turn;
You've so many thing to teach us – how to laugh and how to cry;
And we know that there will be those times
When you will wonder why.

We will always be here for you –
When you're happy or you're sad;
We'll be here for you when things go well,
And when times are good or bad;
You're Mummy's brand new angel and we all want you to know
That you've brought magic to our world –
A brand new light to glow.

So, welcome little Baby: you are loved so very much,
And we cannot wait to meet you, kiss your cheeks
And feel your touch;
You're Mummy's brand new angel,
You've given our hearts a lift;
Your Mummy's little miracle, a wonderful new gift.

Ruth Kilian

The Cuckoo

(Dedicated to my grandsons Kyle, 4 years old, and Oliver, 1 year old)

The cuckoo is such a peculiar bird, she has funny habits, she's
quite absurd.

One day whilst out flying amongst the tall trees,
she spotted a wee, tiny nest.
Because she's so lazy and won't build her own,
She decided to take it as her temporary home.

The poor little bird that had built her warm nest,
decided to put up a fight.
She had no intention of letting that bird
settle down with a bed for the night.

With a great deal of effort and a flapping of wings
and without even taking a rest,
she flew down and pecked her several times,
but that cuckoo would not leave her nest.

After several minutes she attacked once again,
but she knew her efforts would all be in vain,
so she decided to leave her and let her remain,
in her wee, tiny, small, little nest.

The cuckoo she watched the small bird fly away
and into the nest a large egg did she lay,
and as she flew off and left that small, tiny nest,
her newly-laid egg rolled down with the rest.

That small, tiny bird hadn't flown far away,
for she'd no intention to leave.
So she flew back again and this time she'd remain,
for she had a small task to achieve.

After several days, an egg it has hatched,
but the poor little bird doesn't know,
that the task she'll achieve is a cuckoo to feed,
whom she'll care for and think as her own.

That small, tiny fledgling although he was blind,
he could tell that the other small eggs weren't his kind.
It is part of his nature when put to the test,
by instinct alone, he'll remain in the nest.

With tremendous great effort he pushes those eggs up to the top
of the nest
each one in their turn he will take in his stride
as he pushes them out and over the side.
For such a young fledgling it's a very hard test,
that he has to achieve to remain in the nest.

Not once to that bird did it ever occur
That the small, tiny fledgling would grow bigger than her.
The demands of the cuckoo grew constant and loud,
as that poor foster mother flies up in the clouds.

She flies amongst hedges and rivers so bright
in her long busy search for a nice tasty bite.
Searching each day and into the night,
constantly searching, in perpetual flight.

His mother is waiting high up in the sky,
she's been watching his progress as he's learnt how to fly.
And now he will join her way up in the sky, for nature has had
her reward,
he's another new cuckoo, a peculiar bird, with unusual habits
and quite absurd.

M J Hollands

They Knew They'd Not Been Kidded

'I don't quite get question three -
Nor really question four -
In fact, there are words on there
I've never seen before!'

The teacher looked in pained surprise
To them who stood before.
'Oh dear,' said teacher X -
'It's because your reading's poor.'

'I don't like reading,' said pupil A,
'I find it such a bore!
I've never been to the library -
Not even to its door.'

'I cannot do it -
I just don't know!
I won't try anymore
My head is spinning from the strain
And it feels quite sore!'

Ken Clifford

The Donkey

I have been called a silly donkey in my time
At first this hurt and made me very sad,
But on reflection I felt privileged and glad,
For this little animal proudly carried our Saviour in His time.

To the stable on a cold winter's night
The little donkey carried Mary, safe and sound,
Into Bethlehem where the snow lay on the ground,
Then to keep the infant warm, he breathed with all his might.

On the donkey's back there is a cross for all the world to see,
A mark of honour he earned from above, because of you and me.
Then on Palm Sunday, loyal as ever, he gamely toed the line,
As he lovingly carried Christ upon his back for the very last time.

Angela Moore

No More Droppings

Nibble droppings down upon
A useless bag of tell
Some you win, some you lose
Even the crumbs cannot tell
Until it all does crumble
Upon the crummy floor
The nibble droppings
Which will be
Not droppings anymore.

A E Jones

Who Painted The Rainbow?

Who painted the rainbow
High up in the sky?
Who painted the rainbow
It wasn't you or I.
Could it be Joseph Turner or Goya
Who passeth by?
No, God painted the rainbow
To brighten up the sky.

K E Morrison

Robin Redbreast

Little robin redbreast
Darting to and fro
Looking out for titbits
Amongst the trodden snow.

Turning over fallen leaves
For insects hiding there,
With bobbing head and wagging tail
He looks so devil-me-care.

One can see why he's on Christmas cards
By his redbreast that is shown
As this is said to be our Saviour's blood,
In stories that are known.

The birds along with human life
Are all of God's creations,
So it is no mystery that we find
A Christian love for conservation.

Lachlan Taylor

Moonlight Magic

From hillside perch I gaze in awesome wonder
Through the dark shroud of night -
The stillness of the hushed earth cradled humans into quiet rest
A light breeze rustled the autumn skirts of tall trees
Lifting graceful arms, upwards to the starlit sky.
Sharp cry of owl pierced, knife-like, across hedged fields,
The ringing of his voice resonating, calling for his
mate's response.

Clouds scudded by, suddenly revealing the moon's silver light
Her gleaming face now piercing the dark curtain of night.
Her soft beam gleamed on the still lake below -
A mirror of water reflecting the beauty of her face.

Then quickly ran the rabbits, soft, swift-footed, to and fro –
Their little eyes gleaming, noses twitching,
Picking the choicest green food from fields and farms, while
humans slept
Close by, a slow but sturdy hedgehog strutted by
Ambling along the hedge-side, his sharp mouth opening
for hidden prey.

Far above, I gaze into the sky, it's dark vault pattern'd with
little jewelled stars
What mystery lies hidden there, far from us mortals;
A hemisphere of life, unfathomed creation, explored, but not
yet known
Creator God, how small we are before your wondrous Throne.

Kay Rowley